A MIEN FAMILY

A MIEN FAMILY

By Sara Gogol

⌐ Lerner Publications Company ◆ Minneapolis

The interviews for this book were conducted in 1995.

This book is available in two editions:
Library binding by Lerner Publications Company
Soft cover by First Avenue Editions
241 First Avenue North
Minneapolis, MN 55401
ISBN: 0–8225–3407–X (lib. bdg.)
ISBN: 0–8225–9745–4 (pbk.)

LIBRARY OF CONGRESS CATALOGING-IN-PUBLICATION DATA

Gogol, Sara.
    A Mien family / by Sara Gogol.
        p. cm. — (Journey between two worlds)
    Summary: Describes the experiences of one Mien family driven from their home in Laos and moved to a new life in Portland, Oregon.
    ISBN 0–8225–3407–X (lib. bdg.)
    1. Yao American families (Asian Americans)—Oregon—Portland—Case studies—Juvenile literature. 2. Yao Americans (Asian Americans)—Oregon—Portland—Case studies —Juvenile literature. 3. Refugees, Political—Oregon—Portland—Case studies—Juvenile literature. 4. Refugees, Political—Laos—Case studies—Juvenile literature. 5. Portland (Or.)—Social life and customs—Juvenile literature. [1. Yao Americans (Asian Americans) 2. Refugees.] I. Title. II. Series.
F884.P89Y36 1996
306.85'08995079549—dc20   95-48473

Manufactured in the United States of America
1 2 3 4 5 6 – JR – 01 00 99 98 97 96

AUTHOR'S NOTE

I want to thank Ta Jow and Farm On Saechao for agreeing to have their family be the subjects of this book. Ta Jow and Farm On, and their three oldest children—Mey Fam, Cheng Fam, and Muang Fow—shared many memories of past experiences and feelings about their present lives.

The entire Saechao family, including younger sons Nai Chow, Sarn Jow, Sou Chow, and Lou Chio, were willing to be photographed on many occasions. Megen Saechin and Eric Saetern also agreed to photos, as did Nai Yien Saepharn and others at two Mien weddings. The Saechao family's relatives—Lio Kouang, Mouang Fou, Fou Poo, Chieo Poo, Nai Poo, and Chiew Song Saechao—allowed themselves and their children to be photographed.

Seng Fo Chao translated for Ta Jow and Farm On and also explained a great deal about Mien culture and history. His article, entitled "The Iu-Mien and Their History," provided essential historical information.

Finally, Elaine Carter spent many hours taking the present-day family photographs as well as pictures of Portland scenes and two Mien weddings. Elaine's thoughtfully composed photos were invaluable in helping to illustrate the lives of the Saechao family.

SERIES INTRODUCTION

 What they have left behind is sometimes a living nightmare of war and hunger that most Americans can hardly begin to imagine. As refugees set out to start a new life in another country, they are torn by many feelings. They may wish they didn't have to leave their homeland. They may fear giving up the only life they have ever known. Many may also feel excitement and hope as they struggle to build a better life in a new country.

People who move from one place to another are called migrants. Two types of migrants are immigrants and refugees. Immigrants choose to leave their homelands, usually to improve their standards of living. They may be leaving behind poverty, famine (hunger), or a failing economy. They may be pursuing a better job or reuniting with family members.

Refugees, on the other hand, often have no choice but to flee their homeland to protect their own personal safety. How could anyone be in so much danger? The government of his or her country is either unable or unwilling to protect its citizens from persecution, or

Violence has driven many Mien from Laos, a country in Southeast Asia.

7

Small villages dot the mountains of Laos.

cruel treatment. In many cases, the government is actually the cause of the persecution. Government leaders or another group within the country may be persecuting anyone of a certain race, religion, or ethnic background. Or they may persecute those who belong to a particular social group or who hold political opinions that are not accepted by the government.

From the 1950s through the mid-1970s, the number of refugees worldwide held steady at between 1.5 and 2.5 million. The number began to rise sharply in 1976. By the mid-1990s, it approached 20 million. These figures do not include people who are fleeing disasters such as famine (estimated to be at least 10 million). Nor do they include those who are forced to leave their homes but stay within their own countries (about 27 million).

As this rise in refugees and other migrants continues, countries that have long welcomed newcomers are beginning to close their doors. Some U.S. citizens question whether the United States should accept refugees when it cannot even meet the needs of all its own people. On the other hand, experts point out that the number of refugees is small—less than 20 percent of all migrants worldwide—so refugees really don't have a very big impact on the nation. Still others suggest that the tide of refugees could be slowed through greater efforts to address the problems that force people to flee. There are no easy answers in this ongoing debate.

This book is one in a series called *Journey Between Two Worlds*, which looks at the lives of refugee families—their difficulties and triumphs. Each book describes the journey of a family from their homeland to the United States and how they adjust to a new life in America while still preserving traditions from their homeland. The series makes no attempt to join the debate about refugees. Instead, *Journey Between Two Worlds* hopes to give readers a better understanding of the daily struggles and joys of a refugee family.

These Laotians live in a refugee camp in Thailand, a country that borders Laos to the west.

 There's usually something happening in the Saechao family's apartment in Portland, Oregon. At 10 o'clock on a Friday morning in late June, the four youngest boys, Nai (10), Sarn (8), Sou (7), and Lou (5), sit together on a couch facing the TV. They're all watching *The Sandlot*, a movie about American kids and baseball.

Cheng, the oldest brother, is 16. Cheng will be a junior at Madison High School in September. Today he watches the movie, too, and laughs along with his younger brothers at the funny parts.

It's summer vacation and Muang, the second oldest daughter, likes to sleep late when she can. Muang is 13 years old, and in the fall she'll be in the eighth grade at Gregory Heights Middle School. When Muang comes downstairs today, she has a sleepy expression on her face. Yesterday she went strawberry picking, and she had to get up very early in the morning.

The youngest members of the Saechao family—(from left to right) Nai, Sarn, Sou, and Lou—*crowd onto the family's couch to watch a movie.*

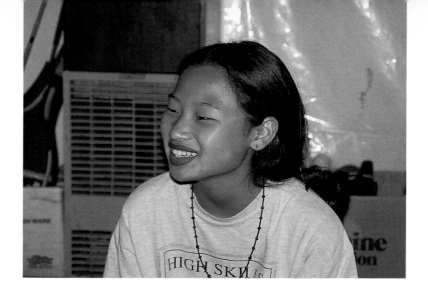

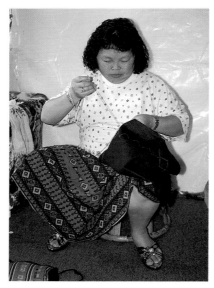

Farm On (above) *keeps her hands busy with embroidery work. Her second oldest daughter is Muang* (right).

The oldest daughter, Mey, is 18 and has just graduated from Benson High School. For the past few days, she's been away on a trip to Mexico. Farm On Saechao, the mother of the family, is busy with household chores. After awhile, she begins to work on some embroidery. Using brightly colored thread, she makes many tiny stitches on a square of black cloth.

The Saechaos are refugees from Laos, but they do not belong to the majority Lao ethnic group. They are part of the Mien ethnic group. Many other Mien people live in Portland, and today is a special day for some of them. This Friday is the first day of a three-day Mien wedding. Family and friends will come together to celebrate with music, chanting, and a bowing ceremony for the bride and groom.

Ta Jow, the father of the Saechao family, has already been at the wedding this morning. He comes home for a few minutes to get chopping boards and a sharp knife. Ta Jow will help cut up meat for the meals the wedding guests will eat.

Last summer Muang and Cheng assisted the bride and groom when their cousin got married. Muang and Cheng aren't planning to attend this weekend's wedding, but Muang may go to another one soon. "It's my friend's sister's wedding," she says.

Cheng, the oldest Saechao son, holds his young cousins.

Farm On and Ta Jow (right) *dress in the traditional clothes many Mien wear to weddings. According to Mien custom, the groom participates in a bowing ceremony* (facing page left) *and the bride wears an elaborate headdress* (facing page right).

Cheng and Muang wore traditional Mien clothes at the wedding last summer. Most of the time, however, they don't like to wear Mien clothes. "They're heavy and hot," Cheng explains.

When Muang describes the traditional turban, or headdress, she says it's "like a mushroom." She wouldn't want to wear it to a wedding or to school. "It's funny," Muang adds, "I wouldn't even want to wear it in the house. It's embarrassing." Muang has mixed feelings about Mien customs.

Born in a refugee camp in Thailand, Nai (above, with Farm On) *was just a baby when his family came to the United States.*

The Saechao family came to the United States in 1986. Mey was almost 10 years old, Cheng was 7, and Muang was only 4. Mien families in Laos and Mien families in the United States lead very different lives. Mey, Cheng, and Muang follow some Mien customs, but they also have many American ideas.

 The Saechao family made a long and difficult journey to come to the United States. Ta Jow and Farm On first met in a refugee camp in Thailand, after each had escaped separately from Laos. When they met, Farm On already had three children. Ta Jow and Farm On's first child together was born in the refugee camp, where the family spent several years before they were able to immigrate to the United States.

Like the Saechaos, other Mien people came to America as refugees. But these refugees were not the first Mien people to move their homes from one place to another. Throughout history, the Mien have made many journeys.

The Mien were originally from China. They believe that about 3,000 years ago, their ancestors controlled part of China. Chinese history books mention a Mien king named Pan Wang (or Bien Hungh in the Mien language). Pan Wang ruled in southwestern China 2,800 years ago.

For centuries, China was divided into many small kingdoms controlled by local warlords, or military leaders. Each leader had strong ties to the Chinese king. Fighting between kingdoms over land and power was common. The Mien faced attacks and also waged their own attacks against Chinese kings and warlords for nearly 3,000 years, from 700 B.C. to A.D. 1949.

After 700 B.C. Chinese rulers forced the Mien into mountainous areas in the south. Here the Mien were farther away from centers of power and less able to create problems for Chinese kings.

The Mien grew rice and other crops in the highlands. But many times the Chinese army drove the Mien to new areas, often killing Mien women, children, and soldiers. During one period in the A.D. 1200s, tens of thousands of Mien, including babies, were killed.

Throughout the history of China, many Mien have worked on important building projects, such as irrigation systems.

To escape persecution, some Mien moved to Laos, Vietnam, and other countries in Southeast Asia in the 1500s. In Laos, where the Saechao family comes from, almost all of the country is mountainous and covered with thick forests, or jungle. In the west, along the Mekong River, lies the country's only lowland region. The ethnic Lao live on this plain, while the Mien and other minority groups have settled in the highland regions. The climate in the lowland is hot, with a rainy season and a dry season each year, but the highlands are somewhat cooler.

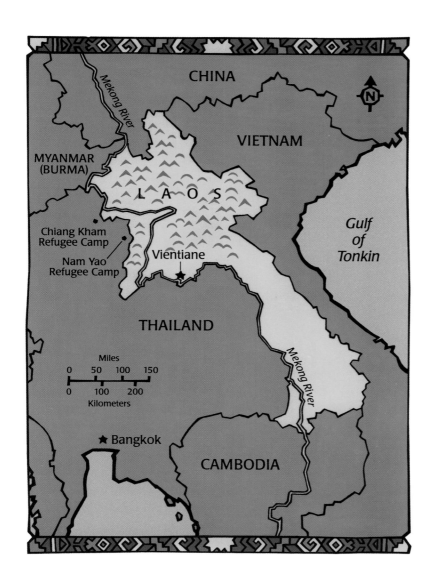

The Mien live in northern and central Laos, (left), where rolling mountains (facing page) dominate the landscape.

The Mien plant and harvest their crops by hand.

The Mien lived in the highest parts of the mountains in northern and central Laos. Their method of farming involved cutting down trees and brush, burning the area to clear it, and then planting. They grew rice and other crops such as squash, beans, and poppies. The men made beautiful silver jewelry and the women embroidered intricate designs on shirts, pants, and hats.

The lives of the Mien people in Southeast Asia were not disrupted until the early 1960s, when civil war broke out in Laos. The war in Laos quickly became part of a larger regional conflict known in the United States as the Vietnam War. Groups that favored a Communist style of government fought against those opposed to Communism.

Supported by the United States, the Royal Laotian government opposed Communist forces. An anti-Royalist group in Laos known as the Pathet Lao received military aid from North Vietnam, a neighboring Communist country. The United States recruited, trained, and paid Mien men and teenage boys to fight against the Pathet Lao.

The war affected Mien people's lives in many ways. Mien boys as young as 12 years old fought in the U.S.-supported army. Women lost their husbands, brothers, and sons. Children lost their fathers. The Pathet Lao burned storages of rice and bombed villages. Often whole villages had to move to safer areas.

In 1975 Pathet Lao forces won the war in Laos. Because the Mien had fought against the Communists, they became targets for persecution. The Pathet Lao began arresting Mien who had participated in the war, first the military leaders and then ordinary soldiers. Some were executed. Others were sent to Communist work camps, where they were forced to work very hard and received only meager food rations. Many died in the camps. Sometimes the Pathet Lao killed whole families in their villages. Some villages were bombed even after the war.

To escape the danger, families and even entire villages began to flee Laos. Many Mien faced a long

The Royal Laotian Army (right) *enlisted many Mien to fight.*

These Mien boys escaped to a refugee camp in Thailand in the late 1970s.

journey through the jungle. Thick underbrush, flooded streams, and sickness made the trek difficult. The refugees carried their few belongings on their backs and traveled as quietly as they could.

Pathet Lao soldiers patrolled the jungle. When they spotted people trying to flee, the soldiers pursued them. Pathet Lao soldiers shot or bombed Mien people in the jungle or as they crossed the Mekong River into Thailand.

About two-thirds of the Mien population in Laos managed to escape. They had originally hoped to settle in Thailand, but the Thai government didn't permit this. Instead Mien refugees had to spend years in Thai refugee camps before they were allowed to immigrate to New Zealand, Canada, France, and the United States.

Some refugees did not want to go to the United States because they had heard rumors of people-eating giants in America. But large numbers of Mien refugees eventually came to the United States. Most of them settled on the West Coast. In 1995 about 22,000 Mien lived in California, 2,000 in Oregon, and 1,500 in Washington.

Many Mien people still live in China, where they are often called Yao. But the Mien themselves prefer the name Mien. That is the term most commonly used in the United States. In 1987 Mien people from several countries met and decided the full name for their people would be the Iu-Mien.

MANY NAMES, ONE PEOPLE

In China Mien people are usually called Yao. But around 1500, when the Mien moved to Guangdong Province in China, the people there mispronounced Yao as Yiu. The Mien themselves began to use that pronunciation.

In written Chinese, symbols called ideograms or characters are used to represent ideas. This is different from the English system, in which letters represent sounds. Many Chinese wrote Yao or Yiu with the character that signifies *dog*. The Mien were also called Man, which means *barbarians* or *savages*. But Mien people disliked these names and preferred to call themselves the Mien, which means *the humans*.

In 1949 Chairman Mao, the leader of China, recognized the help Mien people had given his armies. He changed the ideogram used to write Yao or Yiu to one that means *kings*. The Mien were happy the Chinese government now respected them like kings rather than treating them like dogs.

KING	*wang* or *guo wang*	王 or 国王
DOG	*gou*	狗

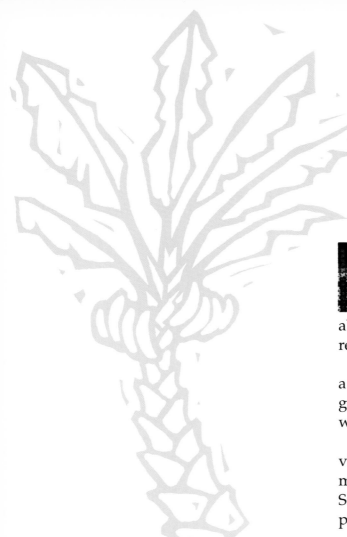

Ta Jow Saechao was only 15 years old when he left his mountain village in the late 1960s and joined the U.S.-supported army to fight against the Pathet Lao. He had no choice about becoming a soldier. "If I refused, I would be arrested," he explains now.

Mien soldiers camped in the mountains for a year at a time. For safe places to sleep, they dug holes in the ground, put leaves on the bottom and covered the top with logs.

Ta Jow was a soldier for about nine years. He still has vivid memories. "On one of our missions there was so much smoke I could hardly breathe," Ta Jow recalls. Small bombs called C-4s had been dropped from planes.

Ta Jow cannot forget a battle one night in which 20 to 30 fellow comrades were killed. Another time a bomb landed so close to Ta Jow that the noise damaged his right ear. "After that bomb, I can't dive underwater," he comments. The water pressure is too painful against his eardrum.

When the war ended in 1975, many Mien soldiers had to escape from the Pathet Lao. "They chased us all the way to the Mekong River," Ta Jow remembers. "Then we had nowhere to run but across the river and into Thailand." Ta Jow knew that if he didn't leave Laos, he would be arrested.

Wearing his uniform, Ta Jow went to China in 1981 for training and supplies.

Ta Jow laughs now about the trick he used to escape. He stole a blank permission form and filled it out to make it seem as if he had official government permission to cross the border. Then he was taken across the Mekong River by motorboat.

Ta Jow lived in Thai refugee camps until 1980, when he joined a group of fighters trying to retake Laos from the Pathet Lao. Ta Jow and other men escaped from the refugee camp and went back to Laos to fight.

Ta Jow even went to China in 1981 along with other Laotian soldiers because the Chinese had promised to help them with supplies and arms. To get there, Ta Jow remembers, "We walked for about one month in the jungle." When he and his fellow soldiers were on the return trip from China, they went days at a time with nothing to eat. One week they ate only fruit and leaves. The soldiers were unable to defeat the Pathet Lao, so Ta Jow returned to a refugee camp in Thailand.

Ta Jow tells how he tricked officials into taking him across the Mekong River to Thailand.

Mey (above) *remembers bits and pieces of her life in Laos, such as the type of house her family lived in* (left).

 Ta Jow Saechao left Laos in 1975, but Farm On had to wait much longer to flee. She wasn't able to leave until 1981. "I tried so many times to escape, but I just could not find a way," Farm On says.

Mey, Farm On's oldest daughter, can still picture a little bit of their life in Laos. "To me it's like a dream that I dreamt a long time ago. I remember there was a tamarind tree, and my aunt went and picked some for me." Tamarind is a fruit that grows in Laos.

"I sort of remember our house," Mey adds. It was built of wood but its roof was made from thick layers of grasses.

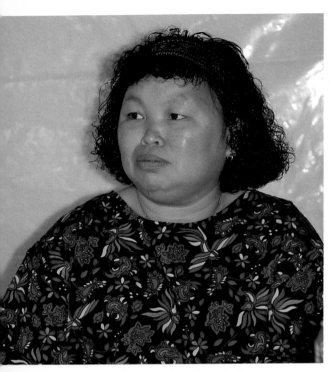

To avoid arrest by the Pathet Lao, Farm On had to leave Laos suddenly.

One day Mey and a slightly older boy were walking along a trail through the jungle to where her parents were working. Mey and the boy had heard about wild elephants that lived in the mountains. "We thought that elephants were going to chase us, and we got little sticks in our hands to chase the elephants away." Mey smiles when she adds, "I don't know how good that stick would be if the elephants would chase after you."

When Mey was about five and her brother Cheng was about three, their mother was forced to leave Laos. One day, when Farm On and another woman were looking for flowers in the jungle, they encountered a family who was escaping from Laos. "The family begged us not to let anyone know," Farm On explains. They even gave her and her friend a little bit of money.

When the family reached Thailand, a man who worked for the Pathet Lao heard the family's escape story and changed it into a dangerous lie. He told the Pathet Lao that Farm On and her friend were taking money to work against the Laotian government.

Farm On heard that she was to be arrested soon. She knew she would be taken to a work camp, where people had so little food they had to eat things like banana peels to survive. Her only choice was to leave right away.

Before Farm On and her children left, they visited relatives. "My family killed a chicken to eat that night to say farewell. They were all crying. They thought

Farm On and her family escaped on foot through the dense jungle.

that we would not be back together in the future." Farm On was so sad, she says, "The chicken meat I ate, it tasted like I was eating a piece of garbage."

Farm On, her two children, and a younger sister, Fey On, escaped through the jungle. Farm On carried Cheng on her back. "I lost a shoe," Mey remembers, "so I had to walk barefoot." The whole family had to be as quiet as possible so Pathet Lao soldiers wouldn't spot them.

When the family reached the Mekong River, Mey remembers, "We waited for the other family who was going to come with us. It was really bright outside, and my brother was crying he was so scared. Because any minute anyone could turn us in."

Farm On and Fey On cut down banana trees to build a raft. But when everyone got on the raft, it started to sink. It wasn't big enough. Luckily, another family had a bigger raft with room for extra people.

Farm On, Mey, and Cheng got on this raft while Fey On tried to cross the Mekong alone on the small one. Fey On drifted away from the bigger raft.

"She was yelling, 'Please help, sister!'" Farm On recalls. "I encouraged her, 'Please be courageous. You can do it! Keep on rowing!'" Fortunately, Fey On did make it.

"The scariest time in my life was crossing the Mekong," Farm On continues. If Pathet Lao soldiers saw her and her children, they would shoot all of them. But the danger was not over even when they got safely to the Thai side of the river. There, Farm On notes, "Many people were robbed and killed."

On their way to the Chiang Kham refugee camp, Mey saw some people from the United States and was

The family built a wooden raft to cross the wide Mekong River.

frightened because they looked so different from Southeast Asians. "I thought, 'Those are the people who are going to eat us,'" Mey explains, "because they had blond hair, blue eyes, big long noses. We had never seen anything like that."

 Ta Jow and Farm On met each other in the Chiang Kham refugee camp. Ta Jow smiles when he thinks about his first sight of his future wife. "When I first met you," he tells Farm On, "you were like a very tiny stick. If the wind blew by you, you would fall down."

Farm On explains that her previous husband had beaten her so badly with a long piece of firewood that she almost died. She left that cruel man and left the Nam Yao refugee camp, where her daughter Muang was born. Farm On went back to the Chiang Kham camp because in the meantime her mother had escaped from Laos and was living there.

Farm On and Ta Jow got married in Chiang Kham and lived together along with Farm On's three children—Mey, Cheng, and Muang. Mey took care of her younger sister much of the time, carrying Muang in a baby carrier on her back. "She was so cute," Mey says. "She was huge. She was really heavy for me to carry all

Mey (right) *recalls watching out for her sister Muang* (left) *while their family lived in a refugee camp.*

A Laotian woman at a refugee camp in Thailand prepares a meal for her family. Some refugees worked odd jobs in the camps to earn money for food, which was often scarce.

day." Their brother Nai was born in Chiang Kham, where Ta Jow helped his wife give birth because no midwives were available.

Ta Jow and Farm On were happy with their new son and happy to be together. But they still had to face a difficult life in the refugee camp. "It was so rough. The roughest life," Ta Jow says.

The camp was fenced with barbed wire so the refugees couldn't escape. It had many long buildings with metal roofs, and each family had only a very small space inside. There was no privacy for individual families within a camp building. "People just walked through it," Cheng notes.

"The camp was so crowded," Ta Jow adds. "There was not enough water to drink, to do laundry with, and barely enough food to eat."

Many people got sick in the refugee camp. One time Mey spent eight days in the camp hospital. While Farm On was with Mey in the hospital, someone came to tell Farm On that her second daughter, Muang, was very sick as well. "She was in a coma, without any feeling, unconscious," Farm On recalls.

Luckily, both Mey and Muang recovered their health. When Mey was feeling well again, like many other children, she had jobs to do in the refugee camp. "I did a lot of cooking," she says. "In the morning I would wake up at five and try to set the fire on the little stove. And I would go out to the well and get water." Mey used water buckets that she hung from a long wooden stick across her shoulder. Mey and Farm On were also very busy with sewing. The family used the money earned from the sewing to buy food from Thai people.

But Mey also had time to play with camp friends. They played a game called Chinese jump rope, which involved jumping as high as they could over a chain made from rubber bands.

Neither Mey nor Cheng went to the camp school. "I couldn't reach my ears," Cheng explains with a grin. He wasn't able to touch his ear on one side by raising his opposite arm over his head and extending his fingers to his ear, so he was considered too young for school. During the day, Cheng ran around the camp with his friends and played a game with a handmade wooden top. He still has a scar on his face where the top cut him once.

Too young to go to school, Cheng spent his days in the refugee camp playing games with friends.

Muang and Cheng agree that life in the refugee camp was very different from their current life in Portland. "I remember sleeping on the floor. It was like concrete," Muang notes. She can also remember a truck with a big plastic tube that came to pump out the camp toilets. Many people watched the process because they had never seen anything like it in the mountains of Laos, where people did not have indoor toilets.

 The Saechaos knew they couldn't return to Laos, so the family applied to immigrate to the United States. Farm On's older sister, Mey On, had already come to the United States. With the help of a Christian church, Mey On sponsored the family. As sponsors, Mey On and the

These photographs of Ta Jow and Farm On were taken in 1986, when the Saechaos applied to immigrate to the United States.

The Saechaos stayed at a processing camp near Bangkok, a large, bustling city and the capital of Thailand.

church agreed to help get the family settled into their new home. "I was very excited to come to America," Farm On recalls, "because I knew that my sister was here, and her life was better than in Laos and in the refugee camp."

Mey also wanted to come to the United States. "I think I was a little afraid, but I was anxious to come here since my aunt was here," she says.

When the Saechao family received permission from the U.S. government to immigrate, they went by bus to the Phanat Nikhom processing camp near Bangkok, Thailand. They stayed in the Bangkok camp for six months, where both Farm On and Ta Jow studied English. But with all the changes they were facing, it was hard for them to concentrate on learning a new language. "We had bad brains," Ta Jow jokes.

The Saechaos made a long journey (facing page) *to come to Portland, Oregon* (above).

From Bangkok, the family traveled by plane to Tokyo, Japan, then to San Francisco, California, and finally to Portland, Oregon. It was the first time any of them had ever been in an airplane. Ta Jow held the youngest child, Nai, for the entire trip. His wife and Nai were sick most of the time, like many other people.

"I slept all the way," Mey recalls. "I don't remember waking up to eat one meal."

Muang was only four at the time, but she remembers falling off her seat on the plane. "I slipped off," she says, "I was falling off the chair."

In September 1986, the Saechao family arrived in Portland, a medium-sized city built on both sides of the Willamette River. Their aunt had found them an apartment in Northeast Portland, where many other Mien families were living.

The family's new life in America was full of surprises. "Everything was so clean, and the houses were so big," Mey remembers. "When I saw those apartments on the other side of the street, I thought that was my aunt's house, and I thought, 'Whoa, she has a huge house!'" Soon Mey found out that the "huge house" was an entire apartment building.

Cheng and Muang both observed how clean places and people were. Cheng noticed all the cars on Portland streets. He also was impressed by the basketball and volleyball courts in the apartment complex.

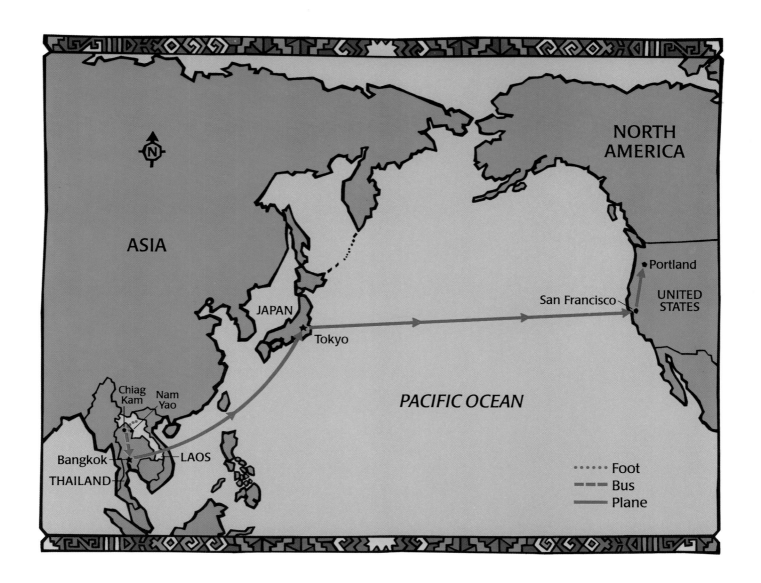

Although it was often difficult to adjust to a new culture, Mey (left, at age 11, holding Sarn) *and Muang* (facing page, at age 6) *liked their new home.*

Paved sidewalks and streets were all new to Mey. In the refugee camp, the ground around buildings was either hard-packed earth or dirt roads. In Portland, on the other hand, "I didn't see hardly any ground," Mey recalls. "It's, like, covered with cement."

Muang liked to jump on the beds in their apartment when they first arrived. "That was the first time I saw a bed," she comments.

Many other things were new and different about the family's life in the United States. Ta Jow and Farm On tried to think positively. "Of course we were homesick," Ta Jow admits, "but we always reminded ourselves that we had no way to return to Laos. So we thought of how to succeed in this country."

The new language, English, was a problem for everyone in the family. Ta Jow studied English at Portland Community College for two months. Then he got a job at the Continental Brass Company, where he polished things like handlebars and handles for boxes.

Mey and Cheng started elementary school, and Muang went to preschool. Going to school for the first time, in a completely new country, was far from easy. After a few months at another school, Mey entered fourth grade at Rose City Elementary School. "It was really strange coming in," she remembers. "I thought I'd never catch up, because all the other kids had studied writing and reading. I could hardly understand anything they'd say."

Muang went to kindergarten at Rice School. Then she started first grade at Rose City Elementary School. When she was in fifth grade at Rose City, she wrote about the refugee camp in Thailand. "I asked my parents and I remembered," Muang explains.

Nowadays Muang only has fragments of memories about the camp. She recalls the heat of the day there, the mosquitoes and other insects, the building her family lived in.

To Muang the refugee camp is most of all a faraway place. "It's like an ancient time or something," she says.

July 4, 1995, is almost nine years since the Saechao family came to the United States. The day is bright and sunny in Portland, and even though it's still morning, people in the Rose City Village apartment complex are already exploding fireworks.

Inside the Saechao apartment, the family is observing a Mien tradition instead of an American one. Guests have come to visit the family. One guest is Seng Fo Chao, Farm On's cousin and one of the leaders of the Mien community in Portland. According to Mien customs, visitors are always offered at least something to drink, and often food as well. Today the Saechao family has prepared traditional Mien food for their guests.

Ta Jow and Farm On are both busy in the kitchen. Mey and her parents bring bowls of food out to a long table. The four younger boys eat in the living room around a low round table while everyone else sits at the big table. One bowl holds cooked greens from squash vines. Other bowls contain pork and bamboo shoots, chopped beef and peppers, and broccoli cooked with beef.

"Please eat," Farm On says. Everyone has their own individual bowl of rice, but people reach with chopsticks to share the food from the other bowls on the table.

Farm On and Ta Jow (left) *cook a special Mien meal, while Mey* (above) *sets the table.*

During the meal, Seng Fo explains that all the children's names have a special meaning. Muang, for example, is associated with love and compassion. When she was born, her parents wanted to say how much they loved her.

Using traditional Mien names is important for cultural identity, Ta Jow feels. "The first thing I do for tradition is to keep our names. None of my children have American names. Only the Mien names."

After the meal is over, the four younger boys rush outside to light fireworks for the Fourth. They obviously enjoy American as well as Mien customs.

All the children now speak both English and Mien. They and their parents find it's not always easy to observe Mien traditions in a new country. For the Saechao family, life in America is a balancing act between the Mien and the American way of life.

In Laos, for example, Mien children would almost always obey their parents. Ta Jow explains that in Laos, if children didn't obey, their parents would beat them. In the United States, he adds, many parents have changed that practice.

The oldest daughter, Mey, respects her parents but she also likes the freedom she has in the United States. "American children," she notes, "have a choice about what to do. They get to make their own decisions most of the time."

After eating the special meal (facing page), *the boys head outside, where Sou* (above) *lights fireworks to celebrate the Fourth of July.*

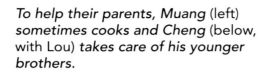

To help their parents, Muang (left) sometimes cooks and Cheng (below, with Lou) takes care of his younger brothers.

Muang believes that if her family were still in Laos, the children would have to do the chores the parents assigned them. In Laos, Muang explains, "You have to work to get food and stuff. So I guess we'd have to do it."

Sometimes when her parents ask her to do a household task, Muang argues with them instead of doing the job. "Muang is the kind of person who does not want to take orders," her father says. "She wants to do it on her own."

Mien children in America are much freer to disagree with their parents than Mien children in Laos, but Mey, Cheng, and Muang still help out. For example, all of them have acted as interpreters when their parents need someone who can speak English well. Cheng and Mey often take care of their younger brothers. Muang answers the telephone for her parents, and when they were away from home for a few days, she watered her mother's garden. Muang also likes to cook sometimes, especially her favorite dish, broccoli and beef.

THE DAUGHTER WHO STOPPED SPEAKING

Mien parents tell this story to their children:

A long time ago, there was a daughter in a Mien family who was rude and disobedient and talked too much. Her mother told her, "In our house you can act this way. But when you get married and go to another family, you'll have to change or you'll be sorry. You'll cry so hard you'll have no more tears to cry."

One day the daughter met a man who married her and took her to his family's home. The daughter remembered her mother's advice. She decided not to talk at all to make sure her husband and his family would love and respect her.

For three years the daughter didn't say a single word. Each day when she fed the pig, she grabbed his ears and pulled him to his food. After she gave birth to a son, she comforted him with her hands.

The daughter's new family thought she was both mute and stupid. The husband said, "It makes no sense for me to stay married to this dumb lady." He decided to return her and the boy to her parents' village.

On the way, they came to a river. A flower was floating on the water. The boy said, "My dad, my dad! Get me the flower." The father ignored his son. Since he was divorcing his wife, he felt that the boy was no longer his. The son cried because his father didn't answer.

The mother hadn't spoken for three years. But when she saw her son crying, she chanted a song: "I have stayed for three years without a single word. They think I am both mute and dumb, so they are sending us back to my parents."

When the husband heard the song, he said, "Oh, my wife! Now you can speak and you can even compose a beautiful song. Please come back home with me again."

But the woman wouldn't change her mind. She said, "You only want someone who is clever. You don't care for people who are in need. You don't have the heart of a human being. I'm sorry," she added. "You have returned me half way. Now my son and I have to go all the way back to the village of my birth."

Sou and Sarn help their father prepare pieces of flour cake in pepper sauce— one of the boys' favorite treats.

 The Saechao family still prepares traditional Mien foods. "Rice is for every meal that we have," Cheng explains. "Breakfast, lunch, and dinner, it's just like all the same. We don't have eggs and toast and then lunch. Breakfast and lunch is just like dinner."

In Laos, meat was a luxury eaten only on special occasions. In Portland, however, the family regularly adds meat or shrimp to their rice and vegetables. The four younger boys enjoy a traditional Asian treat of pieces of flour cake in pepper sauce. But Muang likes to snack on American chips. Once in awhile the Saechaos eat out at a Vietnamese restaurant.

The way the family bedrooms are arranged shows the influence of both Mien and U.S. customs. In Laos, the mother, father, and children under age 12 sleep together in one long bed. In the Saechao apartment in Portland, where there are three bedrooms, the parents share their bedroom with the five- and seven-year-old boys. Until recently Cheng, Muang, and two of their younger brothers shared a room, but now Muang and Mey have a room together.

The Saechaos enjoy spending time together (right). *Sometimes they all go out for dinner at a nearby Vietnamese restaurant* (above).

As soon as Mey leaves for college, Muang says, "I'm going to get my own room." She plans to put up awards and pictures of herself and her friends. Muang is looking forward to having a room of her own.

Ta Jow believes that the United States offers many opportunities for his family. "The first thing the children can do," he says, "is go to school. After they get their education, they can have all kinds of choices."

In Laos it was much more difficult for Mien children to get an education. Before 1960 they did not even go to school, although fathers taught their sons to read and write Chinese characters, which are used in Mien religious texts. After 1960 some Mien boys went to school until they were about 12 years old. Some girls

Mey (above, with her boyfriend Eric) plans to study engineering in college. Muang (right) also hopes to go to college, but for now she's enjoying her classes at Gregory Heights Middle School.

attended classes, too, but they had to fight against parents who believed education would cause girls to give up Mien traditions.

Here in Oregon, Mey received a college scholarship and will be studying engineering this fall at Oregon State University. Cheng would like to attend college as well but thinks he may try a community college first.

Muang already knows she would like to go to college. "If I can afford it," she adds. Right now in school, she says, "I like math, health, and computers, and I like learning about the body." She also enjoys English and social studies and some kinds of writing. "I don't like making up stories," she notes. Sometimes Muang thinks about studying to become a doctor or a nurse when she's older.

Ta Jow and Farm On accept the fact that their children follow both Mien and American customs. The children always speak Mien to their parents, for example, and speak a mix of Mien and English among themselves at home and with their friends. Ta Jow says, "Children need to learn American values in order to succeed in this country."

Both parents worry about the fact that some refugee parents lose control over their children. The Saechao family has relatives living in California, and the family discussed moving there but decided to stay in Oregon. "I think California has too many gangs," Cheng says.

Sarn tries his hand at spinning a traditional Mien top.

49

Ta Jow, who worries that his children might be drawn into gangs, spends as much time as possible with his family.

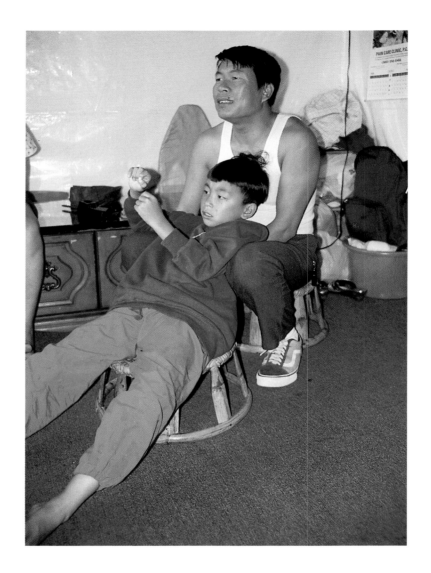

Farm On shows old family photos to Sarn and Sou (right), while Lou (below) relaxes on the couch.

Ta Jow mentions a nephew there who joined a gang, was arrested, and went to prison for six months. "He stole a car and got caught," Cheng explains.

Fortunately, none of the Saechao children have shown any interest in joining a gang. Even so, their parents are still concerned. "That is our number-one fear," Farm On says. "We cannot sleep well whenever we think about other people's children who join gangs."

In spite of their worries about life in the United States, Farm On and Ta Jow are happy their family was able to come here. In many ways, the family has adapted to American life. Yet Mey, Cheng, and Muang agree that both Mien and American cultures are part of their identity. "I'm a mix," Muang says about herself.

In her spare time, Farm On likes to tend to her garden (left) *and embroider traditional Mien designs* (below), *many of which decorate the walls of the Saechao home.*

 Members of the Saechao family keep busy with a variety of activities. Ta Jow cooks and helps take care of the younger children. Farm On does the family cooking, too, and works in her garden. She also embroiders traditional Mien designs—brightly colored geometrical patterns—on squares of cloth or on pants, shirts, and baby hats.

Neither Ta Jow nor Farm On has a job outside the home. Several years ago, Farm On had serious health problems with her heart and lungs, and a doctor advised Ta Jow to stay home to take care of his family. The family has paid bills with help from government financial assistance. Now that Farm On's health is better, both parents may soon be looking for jobs.

The two oldest children, Mey and Cheng, earn their own money from after-school jobs. Mey is a waitress and Cheng washes dishes at a nearby retirement center. In the summer, Muang picks berries to earn spending money.

The Saechao family enjoys having time together. Farm On and Ta Jow tell their children stories about life in Laos. Ta Jow likes playing games with his children as well. "I play cards with them," he says, "and I play ball games with them, and also games like puzzles."

Every Sunday the Saechao family attends the East Side Church of Christ. Many Mien in the United States still follow their traditional religion, which combines a belief in spirits of ancestors and of the natural world with Chinese Taoist beliefs. Many other Mien families have converted to Christianity, but they still participate in traditional celebrations such as weddings and the Mien New Year.

Sarn plays with his new pet—a young chick.

Spending time with relatives is another tradition Mien families keep in the United States. The Saechao children visit their grandmother, aunt and uncle, and cousins, who live in a house nearby. All the Saechao children like playing with their three young cousins.

In their free time, Cheng, Mey, and Muang listen to American music. Muang especially likes rap and soft rock. Cheng and Mey both enjoy sports and sometimes play tennis together. Cheng is on the tennis and soccer teams at Madison High School. Mey was on the tennis and cross-country teams at Benson High School.

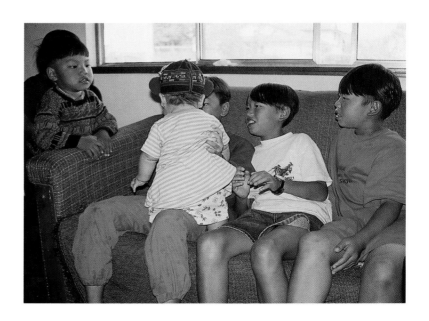

The Saechao children enjoy visiting with relatives, including their grandmother (left), *and their young cousins* (right), *Kao and baby Gen.*

Cheng plays on his high school's tennis team.

Muang enjoys reading many different kinds of books.

Muang is less interested in sports than her older brother and sister. This summer Muang started tennis lessons but dropped them after about a week. She hopes to be on the soccer team when she is in high school. Meanwhile, Muang enjoys other kinds of activities, such as going to movies. Her favorite films, she says, "are comedy, action, and scary movies."

Muang likes to hang out and talk with her friends. And she has a good time shopping with them at a nearby mall. Sometimes Muang and her friends have money to spend. Other times they just look.

Muang is very fond of reading as well. "I recently finished a book called *Rice Without Rain*," she mentions, which is about life in Thailand. She's also read *Children of the River*, a story about Cambodian refugees in the United States. Muang reads many other books on a wide variety of subjects.

The Saechao children don't spend a great deal of time on traditional Mien activities. Muang, for example, was in a Mien dance group for a couple of years but then dropped out. Both Muang and Mey can embroider traditional Mien designs. "My grandma taught me how to do it," Muang says. In Laos embroidery was an important skill for a girl or woman to have. But Muang and Mey are both busy with typical American activities now.

Muang and her friend Megen like to go shopping (right) *or just hang out and talk* (above).

On a Saturday afternoon in late August, the Saechao family drives out to Benson Lake in the Columbia River Gorge. Muang's friend, Megen Saechin, and Mey's boyfriend, Eric Saetern, have come, too. Cheng isn't along because he left on a separate trip that morning.

It's a warm day but not too hot. The sky is clear with only a few high clouds. The family walks along a short trail to a beach shaded by trees. They unroll a straw mat to sit on. Ta Jow gets busy setting up fishing poles for the four younger boys. Eric unpacks two small rubber rafts and a hand pump to inflate them.

Eric, Mey, and Muang all take turns pumping. Ta Jow casts into the lake and then hands a fishing pole to Sarn. "I'm going in that one," Muang says, pointing to the first raft to be filled with air. "Kaboom!" she jokes, as her younger brother Sou takes a turn at pumping up the second raft.

During an outing at Benson Lake, Ta Jow helps Nai bait a fishhook (right). *Later, Muang and Sou splash water to clean off their raft* (above).

Mey and Farm On (right) *watch from shore as Nai and Sou examine crayfish* (above).

Mey lies down on the straw mat. She's tired after a full day of work as a waitress. Muang has more energy. "I'll pump again," she offers for the second raft.

Sarn tries to cast and gets his hook and line caught on an overhanging tree. He and his mother laugh. Muang screws together plastic oars for one of the rafts. She and her friend Megen get into it. "Let's paddle it right in the middle," Muang suggests.

Mey helps push the raft away from shore. Muang and Megen each take an oar and try to row, but all they do is go in circles. "She's not going anywhere," Mey comments.

Eric helps Sarn, Nai, and Sou into life jackets. He and the three boys set off in the bigger raft. Muang and Megen have switched to the smaller raft and finally manage to paddle away from shore. Ta Jow, Farm On, and Mey wade in shallow water looking for crayfish.

Farm On doesn't remember lakes like this in Laos. The biggest river there is the Mekong. But in the rainy season, she explains, "Little creeks turn into big rivers."

Mey likes Oregon much better than the refugee camp in Thailand. Last week she went camping at a lake near Mount Jefferson with Cheng, Eric, and some other young people. "We hiked three or four miles to get there," she says. "It was really peaceful." Mey also likes to go crabbing along the Oregon coast.

Other people take turns with the rafts. The sun sinks lower over the lake, lighting up trees on the cliff behind it. It's almost time to go now. Ta Jow washes off one raft. Muang pushes the second raft into the water and splashes water inside. "This is fun," she laughs.

Muang enjoys rafting. She's been in a canoe and a rowboat, too. She likes being able to do all three activities in Oregon. Here, Muang notes, "We could go to the beach without crossing other states." Once in awhile, her family takes a trip together to the Oregon coast. At Rockaway Beach, Muang says, "We ride really big donkeys, and we go in a boat. At night we make a campfire."

Evening has arrived at Benson Lake, and the Saechao family leaves before it gets dark. Single file, they head back on the narrow trail toward the parking lot. It's been a fun trip for everyone, a good day in their new home in Oregon.

After an afternoon of rafting, Muang and Megen enjoy a snack.

PRONUNCIATION GUIDE*

Cheng (tsehng)
Farm On (farm ohn)
Lao, Laos (LAH-oh, LAH-ohs)
Laotian (lay-OH-shuhn *or* LAH-oh-shuhn)
Lou (loo)
Mekong (may-KAWNG)
Mey (may)
Mien (mee-YEHN)
Muang (mwahng)
Nai (NAH-yee)
Pathet Lao (PAH-theht LAH-oh)
Saechao (say-CHAH-oh)
Sarn (sahrn)
Sou (soo)
Ta Jow (tah choh)
Thailand (TY-land)

* Mien sounds are difficult to translate into English. These pronunciations for Mien words are approximations.

FURTHER READING

Garland, Sherry. *The Lotus Seed.* San Diego: Harcourt Brace Jovanovich, 1993.

Gogol, Sara. *Vatsana's Lucky New Year.* Minneapolis: Lerner Publications Company, 1992.

Graf, Nancy Price. *Where the River Runs.* Boston: Little, Brown, 1993.

Laos in Pictures. Minneapolis: Lerner Publications Company, Geography Department, 1996.

Stanek, Muriel. *We Came from Vietnam.* Niles, IL: Albert Whitman, 1985.

Zickgraf, Ralph. *Laos.* New York: Chelsea House Publishers, 1991.

ABOUT THE AUTHOR

Sara Gogol grew up in Chicago but has lived in Portland, Oregon, for many years. She teaches English at Portland Community College and writes both fiction and nonfiction. In the past she taught English as a second language to refugees from Southeast Asia, including many Mien students.

PHOTO ACKNOWLEDGMENTS

Cover photographs by © Brian Vikander (left) and Elaine Carter (right). All inside photos by Elaine Carter except the following: © Brian Vikander, pp. 6, 7, 8, 18, 20, 27 (left), 29, 30; Panos Pictures/© Liba Taylor, p. 9; North Wind Picture Archives, p. 17; Laura Westlund, pp. 19, 37; Archive Photos/Express Newspapers, p. 21; UPI/Bettmann, p. 22; UNHCR/L. Taylor, p. 32; Robert E. Olson, p. 35; Textile cut-ins embroidered by Farm On Saechao/photographed by Nancy Smedstad